Grades K-2

Scrambled Sentences
PHONICS

40 Hands-on Pages That Boost Early Reading & Handwriting Skills

Seal has tea on the beach.

Seal has tea on the beach.

New York • Toronto • London • Auckland • Sydney
Mexico City • New Delhi • Hong Kong • Buenos Aires

Written and produced by Immacula A. Rhodes
Cover design by Tannaz Fassihi
Interior design by Jaime Lucero
Illustrations by Doug Jones

ISBN: 978-1-338-11298-6

3 4 5 6 7 8 9 10   40   23 22 21 20 19 18

Contents

Introduction 4

Connections to the Standards 4

How to Use the Scrambled Sentences 5

Scrambled Sentences List 7

Scrambled Sentences Activity Pages

Short Vowels

a 8
e 9
i 10
o 11
u 12

Long Vowels: Silent e (CVCe) & Vowel Digraphs

a_e 13
i_e 14
o_e 15
u_e 16
ai 17
ea 18
ee 19
oa 20

Diphthongs, R-Controlled Vowels & Other Variant Vowels

oi 21
ou 22
ow 23
are 24
ar 25
or 26
aw 27
oo (moon) 28

Consonant Blends & Digraphs

br 29
cl 30
cr 31
dr 32
fl 33
fr 34
gr 35
pr 36
qu 37
sk 38
sn 39
sp 40
st 41
sw 42
tr 43
ch 44
sh 45
th 46
wh 47

Scrambled Sentences Template 48

Introduction

Welcome to Scrambled Sentences: Phonics!

The 40 activity pages in this book were developed to give children an engaging and fun way to practice using their phonics knowledge and to put words together to create, read, and write sentences. In addition to boosting early reading and writing skills, the activities also give children lots of opportunities to hone their fine motor and visual skills.

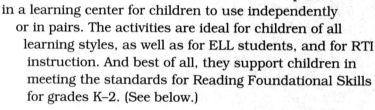

On each page, children cut out and unscramble a set of words to create a sentence that describes a picture. The sentence includes words that target a specific phonics skill for that page, giving children repeated practice in recognizing and reading those words. Once children have arranged and glued the words into a sentence, they write that sentence on the provided line and then color the picture. As they do the activity, children perform a number of tasks, such as cutting, gluing, writing, and coloring, which help build and strengthen their fine motor abilities.

You can use the scrambled sentences with the whole class, in small groups, or as the focus of a one-on-one lesson. You can also place them in a learning center for children to use independently or in pairs. The activities are ideal for children of all learning styles, as well as for ELL students, and for RTI instruction. And best of all, they support children in meeting the standards for Reading Foundational Skills for grades K–2. (See below.)

Connections to the Standards

Print Concepts
Demonstrate understanding of the organization and basic features of print.

Phonics and Word Recognition
Know and apply grade-level phonics and word analysis skills in decoding words.

Phonological Awareness
Demonstrate understanding of spoken words, syllables, and sounds (phonemes).

Fluency
Read with sufficient accuracy and fluency to support comprehension.

Source: © Copyright 2010 National Governors Association Center for Best Practices and Council of Chief State School Officers. All rights reserved.

How to Use the Scrambled Sentences

Materials (for each child)

- scrambled sentence page
- scissors
- glue
- pencil
- crayons

Completing a scrambled sentence page is easy and fun. To begin, distribute copies of the activity page for the phonics skill you want to teach. Point out the words that target that skill on the page and read them aloud. Then have children do the following:

 1 Cut out the word strip at the bottom of the page. Then cut apart the words.

 2 Put the words in order to make a sentence that goes with the picture. Glue the words in the sentence box.

 3 Write the sentence on the line.

 4 Color the picture.

Note: *See the Scrambled Sentences List on page 7 to check the correct word sequence for the sentence on each activity page.*

Teaching Tips

Use these handy tips to ensure children get the most from the scrambled sentence activities.

- **Provide a model:** Display a completed scrambled sentence page. Then demonstrate, step by step, how to complete the activity, including the use of think-alouds to model how to figure out individual words and the sentence.

- **Focus on the target phonics skill:** Have children identify each of the words that contain the phonics skill, read the word aloud, and color the word. In addition, ask them to find and name the items in the picture that contain the target phonics skill. Point out that many of the images picture additional things that include the target sound.

- **Use the clues:** Point out that children can use the picture to help figure out individual words and what the sentence should say. They can also use what they know about sentence features to sequence the words: The first word of a sentence begins with a capital letter and the last word ends with a punctuation mark.

- **Reinforce reading at every step:** Have children read each word after cutting apart the words, before and after gluing the words in place, and after writing the sentence. As children read the sentence, encourage the use of an appropriate inflection for that type of sentence (statement, question, exclamation).

Scaffolding Suggestions

Provide support as children's needs dictate. Here are a few suggestions.

Reading

- Display each word and help children sound it out. You might also read the word aloud and have children repeat.
- Point out each word that targets the phonics skill and ask children to read the word aloud, repeating it several times.
- Provide the correct word order for the sentence. As needed, work individually with children to put the sentence together, one word at a time.
- Model reading the sentence aloud and have children repeat.

Writing

- Have children practice writing the words that contain the phonics skill on the line, instead of writing the full sentence. If needed, write the words on the line in advance and have children trace them.
- Ahead of time, lightly pencil in the sentence on the writing line. Then have children trace the sentence.

TIP

For children with less developed cutting skills, cut out each individual word in advance. Or cut out the word strip and have children cut apart the words.

Ways to Use the Scrambled Sentences

- Learning center activity
- Whole-class instruction
- Small-group instruction
- One-on-one lesson
- Partner activity
- Individual seatwork
- Morning starter
- End-of-the-day wrap up
- Take-home practice

More Uses

- Label a folder with each child's name. Encourage children to place their completed scrambled sentence pages in their folder. Have children use the pages for review and to practice reading.
- Help children compile their pages into a booklet to take home and share.

Customized Scrambled Sentences

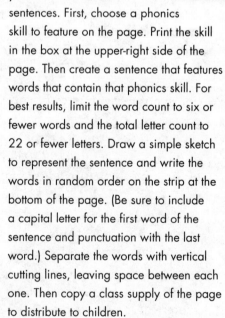

Use the template on page 48 to create your own scrambled sentences. First, choose a phonics skill to feature on the page. Print the skill in the box at the upper-right side of the page. Then create a sentence that features words that contain that phonics skill. For best results, limit the word count to six or fewer words and the total letter count to 22 or fewer letters. Draw a simple sketch to represent the sentence and write the words in random order on the strip at the bottom of the page. (Be sure to include a capital letter for the first word of the sentence and punctuation with the last word.) Separate the words with vertical cutting lines, leaving space between each one. Then copy a class supply of the page to distribute to children.

Scrambled Sentences List

Use this handy list as a reference for checking the correct word sequence for the sentence on each activity page.

ă *(page 8)*
Cat rode a van to camp.

ĕ *(page 9)*
Hen sleds with her pet.

ĭ *(page 10)*
Fish swims in a big sink.

ŏ *(page 11)*
Fox hops across lots of rocks.

ŭ *(page 12)*
Bug juggles plums and nuts.

ā_e *(page 13)*
Ape is late for the plane.

ī_e *(page 14)*
Two mice hide under a vine.

ō_e *(page 15)*
Rose took her bone home.

ū_e *(page 16)*
A cute mule plays the flute.

ai *(page 17)*
Snail paid for a train ride.

ea *(page 18)*
Seal has tea on the beach.

ee *(page 19)*
Sheep plants seeds with a bee.

oa *(page 20)*
Toad gives soap to the goat.

oi *(page 21)*
Pig oinks with a loud voice.

ou *(page 22)*
Mouse looks around at the clouds.

ow *(page 23)*
Cow wore flowers to town.

are *(page 24)*
Hare stares at the squares.

ar *(page 25)*
Park the car in the barn.

or *(page 26)*
Horse eats corn with a fork.

aw *(page 27)*
Hawk sips juice on the lawn.

oo (moon)
(page 28)
Goose wears boots at the zoo.

br *(page 29)*
Bear broke off some bread.

cl *(page 30)*
Clam loves her clown clock.

cr *(page 31)*
Crab uses crayons on her crib.

dr *(page 32)*
Dragon dreams about her drum.

fl *(page 33)*
Fly flips over the flowers.

fr *(page 34)*
Frog picks fresh fruit to eat.

gr *(page 35)*
Greta thinks grass is great!

pr *(page 36)*
The prince wins a prize!

qu *(page 37)*
Duck quacks at the queen.

sk *(page 38)*
Skunk likes to ski and skate.

sn *(page 39)*
Snake tries to sneak a snack.

sp *(page 40)*
Spider slides down the spout.

st *(page 41)*
Steve stands on the stage.

sw *(page 42)*
Dog swings then goes to swim.

tr *(page 43)*
Troy has treats on the truck.

ch *(page 44)*
Chick eats chips and cheese.

sh *(page 45)*
Shark sails the ship to shore.

th *(page 46)*
I have thick and thin pencils.
OR: I have thin and thick pencils.

wh *(page 47)*
Whale blows the whistle.

Name _____

ă

Cut.

Glue.

Write.

Color.

Glue words here.

rode Cat camp. van a to

Scrambled Sentences: Phonics © Scholastic Inc. • page 8

Name _____

e

Cut.
Glue.
Write.
Color.

Glue words here.

sleds | pet. | with | Hen | her

Name _____

Cut.

Glue.

Write.

Color.

Glue words here.

a   big   Fish   swims   sink.   in

Name _____

Ŏ

Cut.
Glue.
Write.
Color.

Glue words here.

Fox across hops of lots rocks.

ŭ

Name _____

Cut.
Glue.
Write.
Color.

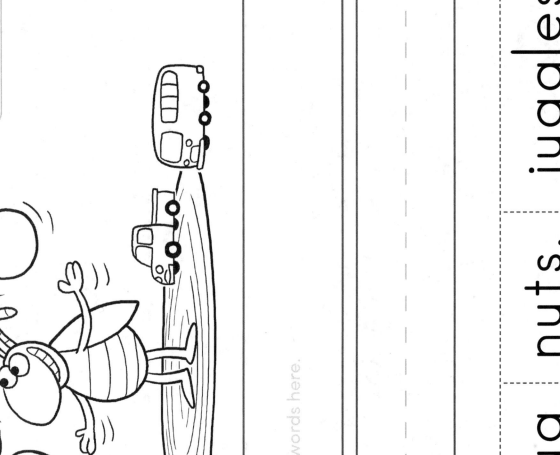

Glue words here.

PLUMS AND NUTS

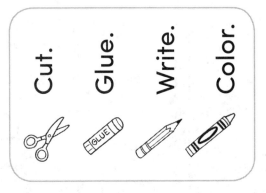

plums | and | Bug | nuts. | juggles

plums

ā_e

Name _____

Cut.
Glue.
Write.
Color.

Glue words here.

the for late plane. is Ape

Name _____

ī_e

Cut. ✂
Glue. 🖊GLUE
Write. ✏
Color. 🖍

Glue words here.

mice Two vine. under hide a

Name _____

ō_e

Cut.   ✂
Glue. [GLUE]
Write. ✏
Color. ▬

Rose

Glue words here.

took   home.   her   Rose   bone

Name _____

ū_e

Cut.
Glue.
Write.
Color.

Glue words here.

Scrambled Sentences: Phonics © Scholastic Inc. • page 16

plays | the | A | cute | flute. | mule

ai

Name _____

Cut.

Glue.

Write.

Color.

Glue words here.

Snail for paid train a ride.

ea

Name _____

Cut.
Glue.
Write.
Color.

Glue words here.

tea | beach. | has | Seal | the | on

Name _____

ee

Cut. ✂

Glue. GLUE

Write. ✏

Color. 🖍

Glue words here.

Sheep | plants | bee. | seeds | with | a

✂

Oo

Name _____

Cut.
Glue.
Write.
Color.

Glue words here.

gives Toad goat. to soap the

Name _____

oi

Cut.
Glue.
Write.
Color.

OINK!

OIL

Glue words here.

voice. oinks loud with Pig a

o

Name _____

Cut. ✂

Glue. 🖍 GLUE

Write. ✏

Color. 🖍

Glue words here.

at the Mouse looks clouds. around

Name _____

ow

Cut. ✂
Glue. 🖍
Write. ✏
Color. 🖍

COWTOWN
2 MILES ⬇

Glue words here.

✂

Cow | to | flowers | wore | town.

are

Name _____

Cut.
Glue.
Write.
Color.

Glue words here.

at | the | Hare | squares. | stares

ar

Name _____

Cut.
Glue.
Write.
Color.

Glue words here.

the   in   car   barn.   the   Park

✂

or

Name _____

Cut.
Glue.
Write.
Color.

Glue words here.

eats Horse fork. with corn a

aw

Name _____

Cut.

Glue.

Write.

Color.

Glue words here.

lawn. sips the juice Hawk on

Juice

Name _____

oo

Cut. ✂

Glue. GLUE

Write. ✏

Color. 🖍

FEED THE ZOO ANIMALS

Glue words here.

at   the   Goose   wears   zoo.   boots

br

Name _____

Cut.
Glue.
Write.
Color.

BREAD

Glue words here.

| off | broke | Bear | bread. | some |

Name _____

Cl

Cut. ✂
Glue. GLUE
Write. ✏
Color. 🖍

Glue words here.

loves | clown | Clam | clock. | her

✂

Name _____

Cr

Cut.
Glue.
Write.
Color.

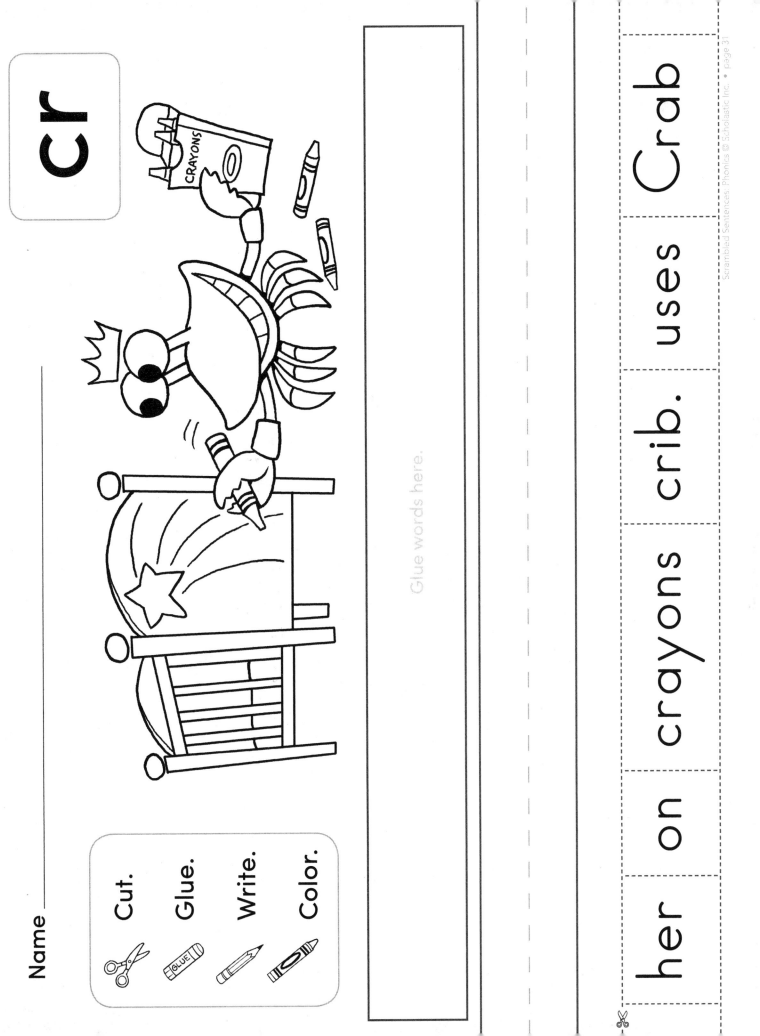

Glue words here.

her | on | crayons | crib. | uses | Crab

dr

Name _____

Cut.
Glue.
Write.
Color.

Glue words here.

dreams | Dragon | her | about | drum.

✂

Name _____

fl

Cut.
Glue.
Write.
Color.

Glue words here.

over | Fly | flips | the | flowers.

Name _____

fr

Cut.

Glue.

Write.

Color.

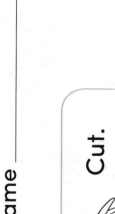

FRESH!

Glue words here.

fresh

eat.

picks

Frog

to

fruit

gr

Name _____

Cut.
Glue.
Write.
Color.

Glue words here.

Greta | grass | thinks | great! | is

pr

Name _____

Cut.

Glue.

Write.

Color.

PRETZEL CONTEST

Glue words here.

| wins | a | The | prize! | prince |

qu

Name _____

Cut.

Glue.

Write.

Color.

Glue words here.

Duck | queen. | the | at | quacks

sk

Name _____

ICE SKATING TODAY

Cut.
Glue.
Write.
Color.

Glue words here.

| and | to | ski | skate. | Skunk | likes |

Name _____

sn

Cut. ✂

Glue. 🖊GLUE

Write. ✏

Color. 🖍

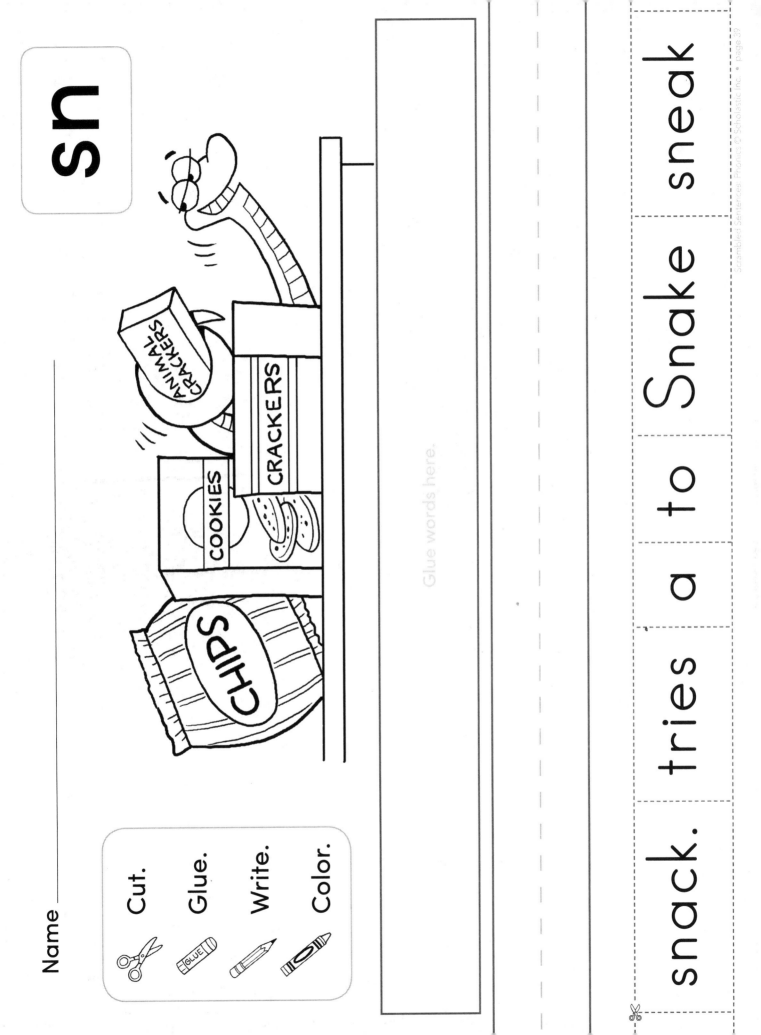

ANIMAL CRACKERS

COOKIES

CRACKERS

CHIPS

Glue words here.

snack.   tries   a   to   Snake   sneak

sp

Name _____

Cut.

Glue.

Write.

Color.

Glue words here.

down

slides

Spider

the   spout.

Name _____

st

Cut.
Glue.
Write.
Color.

Glue words here.

Steve on stands the stage.

sw

Name _____

Cut.
Glue.
Write.
Color.

Glue words here.

then | swim. | goes | Dog | to | swings

BEACH

tr

Name _____

Cut.
Glue.
Write.
Color.

TREAT TRUCK

TROY

Glue words here.

Troy | has | truck. | treats | on | the

ch

Name _____

Cut.
Glue.
Write.
Color.

CHIPS

Glue words here.

cheese.

chips

and

Chick

eats

sh

Name _____

Cut.

Glue.

Write.

Color.

Glue words here.

shore. sails to the Shark ship

th

Name _____

Cut.
Glue.
Write.
Color.

THIN PENCILS

THICK PENCILS

Glue words here.

and | thin | I | have | pencils. | thick

wh

Name _____

Cut. ✂

Glue. 📦 GLUE

Write. ✏

Color. 🖍

Glue words here.

Whale | the | blows | whistle.

Name _____

Cut.

Glue.

Write.

Color.

Glue words here.